DATE	DESCRIPTION	AMOUNT

DATE	DESCRIPTION	AMOUNT

DATE	DESCRIPTION	AMOUNT

DATE	DESCRIPTION	AMOUNT

DATE	DESCRIPTION	AMOUNT

DATE	DESCRIPTION	AMOUNT

DATE	DESCRIPTION	AMOUNT

DATE	DESCRIPTION	AMOUNT

DATE	DESCRIPTION	AMOUNT

DATE	DESCRIPTION	AMOUNT

DATE	DESCRIPTION	AMOUNT

DATE	DESCRIPTION	AMOUNT

DATE	DESCRIPTION	AMOUNT

DATE	DESCRIPTION	AMOUNT

DATE	DESCRIPTION	AMOUNT

DATE	DESCRIPTION	AMOUNT

DATE	DESCRIPTION	AMOUNT

DATE	DESCRIPTION	AMOUNT

DATE	DESCRIPTION	AMOUNT

DATE	DESCRIPTION	AMOUNT

DATE	DESCRIPTION	AMOUNT

DATE	DESCRIPTION	AMOUNT

DATE	DESCRIPTION	AMOUNT

DATE	DESCRIPTION	AMOUNT

DATE	DESCRIPTION	AMOUNT

DATE	DESCRIPTION	AMOUNT

DATE	DESCRIPTION	AMOUNT

DATE	DESCRIPTION	AMOUNT

DATE	DESCRIPTION	AMOUNT

DATE	DESCRIPTION	AMOUNT

DATE	DESCRIPTION	AMOUNT

DATE	DESCRIPTION	AMOUNT

DATE	DESCRIPTION	AMOUNT

DATE	DESCRIPTION	AMOUNT

DATE	DESCRIPTION	AMOUNT

DATE	DESCRIPTION	AMOUNT

DATE	DESCRIPTION	AMOUNT

DATE	DESCRIPTION	AMOUNT

DATE	DESCRIPTION	AMOUNT

DATE	DESCRIPTION	AMOUNT

DATE	DESCRIPTION	AMOUNT

DATE	DESCRIPTION	AMOUNT

DATE	DESCRIPTION	AMOUNT

DATE	DESCRIPTION	AMOUNT

DATE	DESCRIPTION	AMOUNT

DATE	DESCRIPTION	AMOUNT

DATE	DESCRIPTION	AMOUNT

DATE	DESCRIPTION	AMOUNT

DATE	DESCRIPTION	AMOUNT

DATE	DESCRIPTION	AMOUNT

DATE	DESCRIPTION	AMOUNT

DATE	DESCRIPTION	AMOUNT

DATE	DESCRIPTION	AMOUNT

DATE	DESCRIPTION	AMOUNT

DATE	DESCRIPTION	AMOUNT

DATE	DESCRIPTION	AMOUNT

DATE	DESCRIPTION	AMOUNT

DATE	DESCRIPTION	AMOUNT

DATE	DESCRIPTION	AMOUNT

DATE	DESCRIPTION	AMOUNT

DATE	DESCRIPTION	AMOUNT

DATE	DESCRIPTION	AMOUNT

DATE	DESCRIPTION	AMOUNT

DATE	DESCRIPTION	AMOUNT

DATE	DESCRIPTION	AMOUNT

DATE	DESCRIPTION	AMOUNT

DATE	DESCRIPTION	AMOUNT

DATE	DESCRIPTION	AMOUNT

DATE	DESCRIPTION	AMOUNT

DATE	DESCRIPTION	AMOUNT

DATE	DESCRIPTION	AMOUNT

DATE	DESCRIPTION	AMOUNT

DATE	DESCRIPTION	AMOUNT

DATE	DESCRIPTION	AMOUNT

DATE	DESCRIPTION	AMOUNT

DATE	DESCRIPTION	AMOUNT

DATE	DESCRIPTION	AMOUNT

DATE	DESCRIPTION	AMOUNT

DATE	DESCRIPTION	AMOUNT

DATE	DESCRIPTION	AMOUNT

DATE	DESCRIPTION	AMOUNT

DATE	DESCRIPTION	AMOUNT

DATE	DESCRIPTION	AMOUNT

DATE	DESCRIPTION	AMOUNT

DATE	DESCRIPTION	AMOUNT

DATE	DESCRIPTION	AMOUNT

DATE	DESCRIPTION	AMOUNT

DATE	DESCRIPTION	AMOUNT

DATE	DESCRIPTION	AMOUNT

DATE	DESCRIPTION	AMOUNT

DATE	DESCRIPTION	AMOUNT

DATE	DESCRIPTION	AMOUNT

DATE	DESCRIPTION	AMOUNT

DATE	DESCRIPTION	AMOUNT

DATE	DESCRIPTION	AMOUNT

DATE	DESCRIPTION	AMOUNT

DATE	DESCRIPTION	AMOUNT

DATE	DESCRIPTION	AMOUNT

DATE	DESCRIPTION	AMOUNT

DATE	DESCRIPTION	AMOUNT

www.ingramcontent.com/pod-product-compliance
Lightning Source LLC
Chambersburg PA
CBHW072226170526
45158CB00002BA/777